Contents

Young Spirit 6
Esperanza 7
Spirit 8
Little Creek 9
Rain 10
A Leader is Born 11
Make a Spirit Mobile 20
Little Creek Look-Alikes 23
A Spirit That Cannot Be Broken 24
Return to the Homeland Game 37
Love and Friendship 40
Escape 48
The Spirit of Freedom 56
Running Free 59

SPIRIT
STALLION OF THE CIMARRON
Annual 2003

Published by Pedigree Books Limited
The Old Rectory, Matford Lane, Exeter EX2 4PS
E-mail books@pedigreegroup.co.uk
Published in 2002

TM & © 2002 DreamWorks L.L.C.

Young Spirit

Young Spirit was born in the spring, in a field of lush grass and wild flowers, on the open plains of the American West. Filled with wonder at the world around him, the curious young foal amuses his mother, Esperanza, with his playful antics and sense of adventure, as he grows from a restless, carefree colt into a proud and strong stallion.

Esperanza

Spirit's patient and loving mother, Esperanza, is a beautiful and brave Palamino mare who keeps a cautious eye on her bold young colt. As Spirit goes off on his many adventures, Esperanza teaches him which creatures are friends and which may be enemies, preparing him for the day when he takes his place as leader of the herd.

Spirit

As leader of the Cimarron herd, Spirit, a brave and noble mustang, is determined to maintain his freedom at any cost. In the course of his many adventures, he is confronted by men who try to break him, forms a special friendship with a young American Indian, and falls in love with a beautiful paint mare. Through it all, Spirit discovers the true hero inside himself.

Little Creek

A strong and compassionate young Lakota Indian, Little Creek meets Spirit when both are captured by the cavalry. After they make a daring escape together, Little Creek takes Spirit back to his village. As their friendship develops, Spirit meets Little Creek's horse, Rain, and sees for the first time how men and horses can have a relationship based on trust and respect.

Rain

A beautiful and gentle young paint mare, Rain is fiercely loyal to Little Creek. She is very strong-willed and determined to show Spirit the good that surrounds the Lakota village, even as she finds herself falling in love with him. Although she is tempted to run away with Spirit, Rain's instincts bring her back to Little Creek's side when he needs her most.

A Leader is Born

They say the history of the West was written from the saddle of a horse. But it's never been told from the heart of one. Not until now. . . . .

Spirit's homeland was a perfect place for a wild colt to be born. There were wide blue skies and deep red-rock canyons. Tall pines grew in the mountains and clear rivers ran through the rich valleys. It was beautiful.

Spirit was born in the springtime. His mother, Esperanza, laboured hard, lying near the herd, half hidden in the tall grass.

Like all colts, Spirit was awkward and clumsy at first. He wobbled as he walked, staring at everything around him. There were other horses – lots of them. This was his herd, his family. He spent his first summer growing and learning.

By the time the first snows fell, Spirit was swift and strong. When the herd galloped together he could keep up with ease. One day, he went to the lake with the other colts.

As Spirit lowered his muzzle to drink the ice-cold water, he heard a strange sound – a rumbling in the earth.

Astonished, he whirled around to face a wall of huge woolly beasts. Buffalo! Staring down at him sternly, the biggest bull let out a roaring bellow.

Determined not to let the huge animal scare him, Spirit gathered his courage and reared, whinnying at the buffalo in his high, clear colt's voice. The enormous beast blinked, amazed and amused at the bravery of this half grown horse.

Esperanza whinnied from the bank, beckoning for Spirit to come back to the herd. He cantered away, rearing and striking at the air as he topped the ridge, just like a grown stallion claiming his homeland would have done. That was what he wanted one day. He wanted to be the lead stallion of the Cimarron herd.

As indeed, Spirit grew taller and stronger he took his place at the head of the herd. When spring came again, he began to stand watch to make sure no enemies were near. The herd was his responsibility and he did his best to protect it.

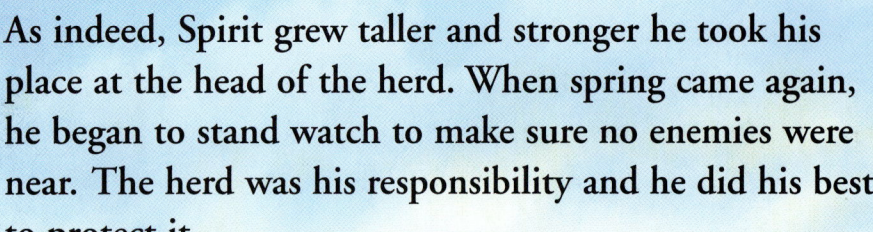

Even with Spirit alert and wary, enemies sometimes managed to come close. One day, when two foals were playing in the meadow, a cougar was slinking silently towards them, staying upwind so that the horses could not scent it.

Furious that this predator had come so close, Spirit charged forward and reared, striking the cat's face with his forehooves. It flinched and snarled, showing its wicked, curved teeth.

The cat sprang without warning, leaping onto Spirit's back. Its claws were long and sharp and Spirit staggered beneath its weight. He tried to throw the big cat off his back, but it only dug its powerful claws deeper into his skin.

Desperate, Spirit vaulted into a dangerous fall, rolling head over heels, crashing onto his back. The cat released its hold and lay still, stunned. Spirit reared, but as his legs crashed to the ground, the cougar ran away.

Later, the herd was relaxed again, the colts playing and delaying bedtime as long as they could. As Spirit passed through the herd, the two colts he had saved from the cougar bounded off, as frisky as ever.

Spirit gave them a stern look and they quieted. He climbed a knoll that gave him a good view of the valley. Then a distant sparkle caught his eye.

It was flickering, like fire, but the twinkling light was tiny. Had a star fallen to the earth? Spirit signalled for his mother to join him and asked her to watch the herd until he could return.

Spirit set off. Whatever the strange new light in their homeland turned out to be, it was his responsibility to find out about it.

Make a Spirit Mobile

You will need scissors, a needle, glue, some strong thread and a disposable chopstick. Adult help is needed when using scissors, needles and other sharp objects.

Trace (or photocopy) and colour the pictures of Spirit and Rain on pages 21 and 22, then carefully cut out all the shapes. Stick the matching shapes together, back to back.

Thread the needle and tie a large knot in the end of the thread. Push the needle through **the top of the heart-shaped picture of Spirit and Rain**, where marked, and join it to the bottom of the shape above, leaving a length of thread between the two, as shown below. Use the needle and thread to attach all other shapes to the chopstick. Tie another length of thread to either end of the chopstick so you can hang your mobile from a hook, or at a window.

Little Creek Look-Alikes

Below are 8 drawings of Little Creek, but only two are identical. Can you find the matching pair? See answer below.

Answer: the matching pair are c and e

A Spirit That Cannot Be Broken

Spirit could smell the unmistakable scent of fire. The young stallion approached the strange glow – it was a fire, but it was small and round, and the creatures around it were funny-looking with odd, patchy coats.

Spirit waited to be sure they were asleep, then stepped forward. If any danger threatened, he would gallop like the wind. But first he wanted to find out what these strange creatures were and why they had come to his homeland.

Spirit made his way slowly towards them. He approached one and dropped his head low to sniff at its face. "Sadie May," it mumbled. "Oh, mmmmmmm… Sadie." Spirit touched the creature's cheek lightly.

The creature puckered its lips and made a squelching sound. It pressed its mouth against Spirit's muzzle. "Ewwww!!!!" two of the others said. The rest stumbled to their feet. "C'mon, men!" one of them shouted.

Spirit wheeled around. He hesitated, then broke into a canter. Shouts followed him, "Look out! He's getting away! Get him!" Spirit galloped faster, then he heard the sound of hoofbeats and glanced back. The men had climbed up onto horses' backs. And they were chasing him!

The idea of a man straddling his back made Spirit grit his teeth. Why would the horses allow it? Spirit was confused, but he wasn't worried. What horse could outrace him carrying a big, heavy, two-legged creature on its back? Spirit began to distance himself from the riders, then realised he had made a terrible mistake. He was in a box canyon, there was no way out.

Suddenly, a rope snaked out and looped over his neck. He saw the herd on a rocky ridge, staring down at him and whinnied a furious warning to Esperanza.

Spirit glared at the riders' mounts, who turned away in shame. "We can sell him to the soldiers," one of the men said. Spirit had no choice but to go with them.

The journey was long and miserable. Crossing the Red Mesas, Spirit scuffed his hooves in the dry, rocky soil, but when he tried to stop, the riders forced their horses to drag him forward. Two days passed as Spirit shuffled along.

The next morning, the men pulled Spirit toward a place so strange that he could only stare. It was surrounded by trees that had been cut and propped upright in a straight line, forming a high fence. The men who had caught him talked to men inside the fence for a long time. These, Spirit understood, must be the soldiers. The soldiers grabbed the ropes and pulled Spirit inside.

As Spirit was pulled forward, he saw that these men had captured other horses, too. They were standing uneasily, lined up and marching in straight rows, with riders on their backs.

Shaking, Spirit reared, unable to contain his fear and anger any longer. Somehow, the straight lines of horses were even more unnatural than the walls and the buildings.

Suddenly, there was a sound like a crack of thunder. Spirit looked up to see a man holding something shiny. He understood that it had made the sound — and that it was dangerous. "What seems to be the problem here, gentlemen?" asked the man.

"We got us a crazy one here, Colonel," a soldier replied. "The army has dealt with wild horses before," the Colonel said, "Induct this animal, Sergeant." The soldiers dragged Spirit forward and tied him to stout posts. "Murphy, he's all yours," said the sergeant.

Spirit felt a tugging at his neck. From the corner of his eye he could see long strands of dark hair lying in the dust. Murphy had cut off his mane! Spirit was furious.

Spirit allowed Murphy to approach him again but, when Murphy suddenly picked up his rear hoof, Spirit unleashed a powerful kick at the man's wide rear end.

The Colonel frowned angrily. "It's time to break that horse." Spirit struggled as the men threw a saddle on his back and the weight of a rider sank down onto the saddle.

Spirit's anger exploded. He rushed out, bucking, circling, twisting hard, kicking high with his hind legs, until the weight of the rider suddenly eased and was gone. A second later, the man hit the dust, hard. Spirit stood for a few seconds, then looked up, ready for the next man. It didn't take long.

He lunged against the pressure of the second rider, reeling and twisting, rearing high, then slamming back down. The rider sailed off his back and through the air.

One thing was obvious. These two-leggeds didn't know when to leave something alone. Spirit threw a third rider, then a fourth, and a fifth and a sixth. As the men hit the dirt, the cavalry horses whinnied and stamped their hooves, cheering him on.

The Colonel scowled and stared into Spirit's eyes. Spirit trembled with rage. Finally the Colonel shouted, "Tie this horse to the post. No food or water for three days."

As the days passed, Spirit's hooves carved a track in the loose dirt around the post. He was hungry, but it was his thirst that bothered him most. He swallowed painfully. Suddenly there was a commotion at the fort gates. "We've got a hostile!" a soldier shouted. The prisoner was gangly, not quite grown, like a three-year-old colt. He stared at the sky as the soldiers tied him to the post. "Hey," the boy said quietly to Spirit as the soldiers walked away. "I'm Little Creek."

During the night Little Creek began to hoot like an owl. Suddenly a sharp object flew through the air and landed at his feet. He kicked it over his shoulder and used it to free his hands.

"How long has the mustang been tied?" asked the Colonel. "Three days, sir," came the reply. The Colonel ordered the sergeant to fetch his crop and spurs, then he climbed on Spirit's back.

The Colonel dug his heels into Spirit's sides, startling him into action. Spirit bucked and twisted, then whirled and fought his way across the corral in a series of body-wrenching leaps. The saddle slid loose. Furious and frantic to be free, Spirit used all his strength to throw the Colonel backwards, out of the corral. Then he threw his weight against the fence, which collapsed.

Spirit turned to see the Colonel striding towards him, holding the shiny thing that made the thundercrack sound, but all of a sudden, Little Creek raced towards the Colonel and knocked him down. Then he jumped onto Spirit's back.

Little Creek grabbed a soldier's rifle and fired at the stable doors. They blew open and the horses rushed out. Spirit headed towards the front gates, and galloped out onto the open plains, the cavalry horses behind him, scattering in all directions.

Return to the Homeland Game

Follow the trail from the soldiers' fort to Spirit's homeland.

A game for two to four players

You will need a dice, plus scissors, glue and some thin cardboard such as a cereal box (or four coloured plastic counters).

Note: adult help is needed when using scissors.

Photocopy, or trace and colour, the counters on page 38 (you may want to glue them to some thin cardboard). You can use four coloured plastic counters instead.

Well done! You are back at your homeland.

74 73 72 71 70

A herd of water buffalo are crossing your path. Miss a turn to let them pass.

69 68 67 66 65 64 63 62 61 60 59 58 57 56 55 54 53 52 51 50 49 48 47 46 45 44 43 42 41 40 39

The Colonel and his men are up ahead. Take a shortcut to 65.

Gallop forward to 49 to escape from the forest fire.

Love and friendship

Little Creek whistled and an instant later Spirit was amazed to see a beautiful pinto mare galloping beside him. Little Creek settled himself on her back. "Rain!" he said, "I knew you would come."

Suddenly Spirit felt ropes drop around his neck. Two young men about Little Creek's age had appeared from nowhere. Spirit tried to free himself, but he was too tired to resist these new captors.

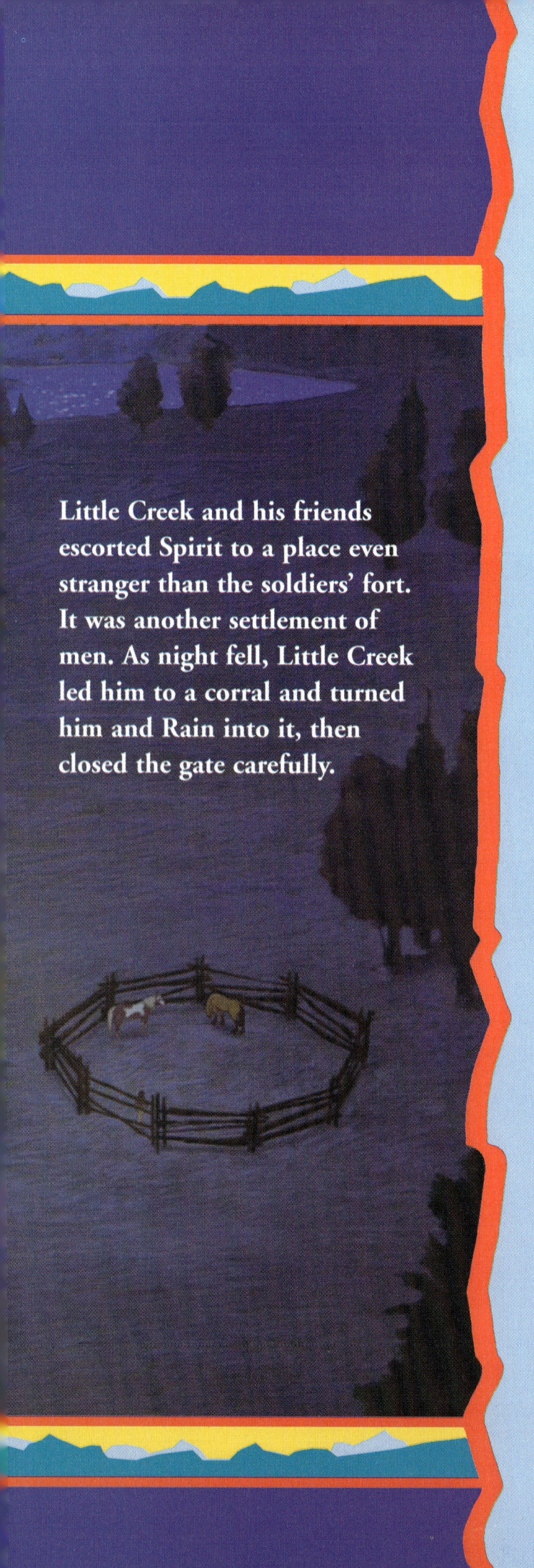

Little Creek and his friends escorted Spirit to a place even stranger than the soldiers' fort. It was another settlement of men. As night fell, Little Creek led him to a corral and turned him and Rain into it, then closed the gate carefully.

The next morning Spirit found a pile of apples in the corral. He began to eat, enchanted by the taste. Then he saw Rain standing across the meadow. As pretty as she had looked by moonlight, the morning sun made her even more beautiful.

Soon Little Creek came to the corral. "Great Mustang," he said respectfully, "Today I will ride you." Spirit whirled and moved away. He liked Little Creek and didn't want to hurt him, but he refused to let himself be ridden.

But Little Creek would not give up. Finally Spirit exploded and he charged Little Creek, who jumped through the fence. Suddenly Rain appeared, her ears pinned back in protective fury. Spirit was stunned. He could not imagine why she would protect a man-colt but he admired her courage.

The next time he came, Little Creek brought Rain into the corral. "Okay, Rain," the boy said, "Let's see if you can teach this mustang some manners." Something slid around Spirit's neck – a rope! The boy tied the other end of the rope around Rain's neck!

Once they were out of the corral, Spirit tried to gallop towards open country but Rain pulled him to a stop. Spirit stood still, furious. He was so close to freedom. And why didn't she want to be free herself?

Rain led Spirit around the village where Little Creek and his people lived. It was clear that Rain cared deeply for Little Creek and the villagers. The horses also seemed content and cared for.

The day was warm, and the horses waded into a wide, still pond to cool off. Spirit wondered if Rain could possibly like him as much as he liked her. Rain turned and met his eyes. Everything he needed to know was in her gaze. She liked him very much. For the first time in his life, Spirit felt torn – he longed to go home but he did not want to leave Rain.

Day after day Little Creek tried to ride Spirit without success. Then one morning, the boy surprised him. "I'm never going to ride you, am I?" he muttered, opening the gate, "It's okay – go!"

Spirit galloped away, but then he veered off to find Rain. He wanted her to become part of the herd he loved. Spirit could tell that she wanted to follow him, but that she also wanted to stay. Suddenly the sound of hoofbeats made him turn. The Colonel and his men were attacking the village!

Rain galloped back into the thick of the battle, looking for Little Creek. When Spirit finally spotted her, she was carrying Little Creek straight towards the Colonel himself. The Colonel raised his gun to fire. Rain reared in terror and the bullet struck her shoulder.

Rain fell sideways into the rushing water and Little Creek was thrown off her back. The Colonel turned to Little Creek and raised his gun again. Spirit ran into the Colonel's horse as the gun went off. The shot went wild and the Colonel fell.

Spirit leaped into the river and positioned himself so that Rain could lay her head on his back, using his strength to keep her head above the fierce current. Then a rushing roar in the distance caught his attention. A waterfall!

Spirit struggled to save himself and Rain, as the current swept them over the falls and the cold water closed over his head. Fighting his way to the surface, he saw Rain lying on the bank. Spirit lay down beside her, willing her to live.

"Hey, there are a couple of horses down here!" Spirit glanced upwards. Soldiers! "Leave the mare," one of them said. "She's not going to make it." Spirit was too exhausted to fight and could only stumble along, as the soldiers dragged him away.

Spirit was cold and scared. He had never seen anything like this huge metal contraption that the men called a train. Shoved inside with all the other horses the soldiers had captured, Spirit hung his head.

When the train stopped, Spirit was astonished at what he saw around him. The grass had been trampled flat and the trees were piled in two long, endless stacks that ran up the slope above him. The soil itself had been gouged and scraped.

Far from the railroad town, Little Creek was walking the strangest path he had ever seen – the path made for the steam-belching train engine. He had seen Spirit being forced into the train and he hoped that if he followed these rails long enough, he would find the proud stallion unhurt, with his heart and his pride still strong.

Escape!

The next morning the men hitched the horses to a massive sled carrying an enormous steam engine. In front of them was a steep hill. "Ready to go!" a man cried out. Spirit struggled to move forward. Inch by painful inch, the horses fought to drag the engine up the rough, uneven slope.

When they reached the top of the hill, Spirit looked over the ridge and blinked. Spread out before him was his homeland. They would cut the trees and scar the earth, just as they had done here. Spirit couldn't let it happen.

Suddenly, he had an idea. He closed his eyes and fell to the ground. The men wrapped a chain around his legs and unhitched him from the rows of exhausted horses. Then, as they dragged him away, Spirit exploded into action.

Spirit galloped back to the sled and kicked apart the pins and locks that held the harnesses. He whinnied, urging the horses to run away. They scattered up over the ridge as the men shouted in panic.

Spirit raced down the hill, then he looked up and his heart almost stopped. The engine was crashing down towards him. Spirit galloped for his life, barely managing to stay ahead of it.

Making a desperate leap, Spirit managed to jump clear of the falling engine, which crashed with a huge explosion at the bottom of the hill.

The crash threw sparks in every direction, like red-gold snow. Spirit whirled and burst into a gallop. The pine forest erupted into flames and the fire spread quickly.

As Spirit leapt to clear a fallen tree, the chain trailing from his neck caught on a broken branch. He dropped to the ground, the chain so tight he could not breathe. Suddenly, Little Creek appeared and cut the branch to free the chain.

Spirit struggled upright and together they fled from the inferno, until their path ended suddenly at the edge of a river gorge. They plunged into the icy water and then, staggered out onto the soft sand.

The next morning, Spirit woke to see Little Creek at the water's edge, bending over to drink. It seemed so long since they had been in the corral, running and dodging as Little Creek tried to ride him. Spirit realised he had missed their games. He nudged Little Creek who fell into the water.

Little Creek ran at Spirit and the two of them leaped and sparred, splashing in the water. Little Creek smiled. "I knew I would find you," he said. A faint sound startled Spirit and he turned to see the Colonel and his men.

The Colonel looked as surprised to see Little Creek and Spirit as they were to see him. "Go! Go! Hah! Get out of here!" Little Creek shouted at Spirit and they both fled at the same instant.

Without warning, Little Creek fell. Spirit galloped on, then slowed. The cavalry men were approaching, but Little Creek had saved his life. As he turned to gallop back, Spirit realised that being forced to carry a rider was different from choosing to save a friend.

Spirit lowered his head so that Little Creek could grasp his mane and swing onto his back. They headed for the mouth of a canyon. In the distance, they could still hear the Colonel shouting, "Split up! Split up!"

Little Creek pulled a dead limb off a tree and, as they passed beneath a narrow arch, he jammed the branch in place. A few seconds later it knocked the soldier from his horse.

The narrow, rocky trail spiralled sharply upwards. Spirit was sure he could outrun the soldiers' mounts in such rough country, but then hoof beats behind him made him whirl around. Another rider was galloping towards them.

The soldier gave Little Creek a vicious shove. The boy gripped Spirit's mane as he fell, his feet hanging over the sheer drop, then he vaulted upwards, kicking the soldier hard so he fell onto the rocky path.

A sharp turn in the path brought Spirit to a sliding halt. His front hooves were poised on the edge of a steep drop. There was a rough incline and he had no choice but to climb it. At the top, they found themselves on a pinnacle of rock. They were trapped. There was no way out.

The Spirit of Freedom

"There they are!" came a shout. Spirit looked down. The Colonel and two soldiers were glaring at them. A bullet whistled through the air close to Spirit. He stared at the far rim of the canyon. It was far from them – too far.

Spirit narrowed his eyes. He might make it if he jumped with every bit of his strength. "Oh, no," Little Creek murmured, realising what he intended to do. Then Spirit leaped forwards with all his strength and all his will.

The ground on the far side seemed to rush up at them. Spirit landed hard and Little Creek spilled forward, sliding on the rocks. For a long moment they both lay still, gasping for breath, their eyes closed. Then they stood up together, swaying on their feet, looking back at the impossibly wide chasm they had leaped. The Colonel and soldiers stared in disbelief.

One of the soldiers lifted his rifle but the Colonel pushed the rifle barrel down. He met Spirit's eyes and he nodded. Spirit lowered his muzzle, imitating the man's gesture. It was a signal of truce, of respect. The battle between them was over.

Following the scent of campfires, Spirit headed towards Little Creek's village. Suddenly, Little Creek raised his fingers to his lips and blew. Spirit heard hoofbeats and was astounded to see Rain galloping towards them.

Rain nuzzled Spirit's neck. Little Creek smiled, "You will be in my heart always," he told her. "Take care of her, Spirit-Who-Could-Not-Be-Broken." Little Creek put his arms around Spirit's neck. "I'll miss you, my friend."

Whinnying a farewell, Spirit and Rain cantered away. They ran for several days and nights until they reached a knoll overlooking Spirit's homeland. Below them, they saw the Cimarron herd.

The news of Spirit's return quickly spread through the herd and all the horses began to celebrate, rearing and tossing their heads. Spirit and Rain led them in a gallop across the wide valley, their hooves echoing like thunder, their hearts joined in their shared love of freedom.